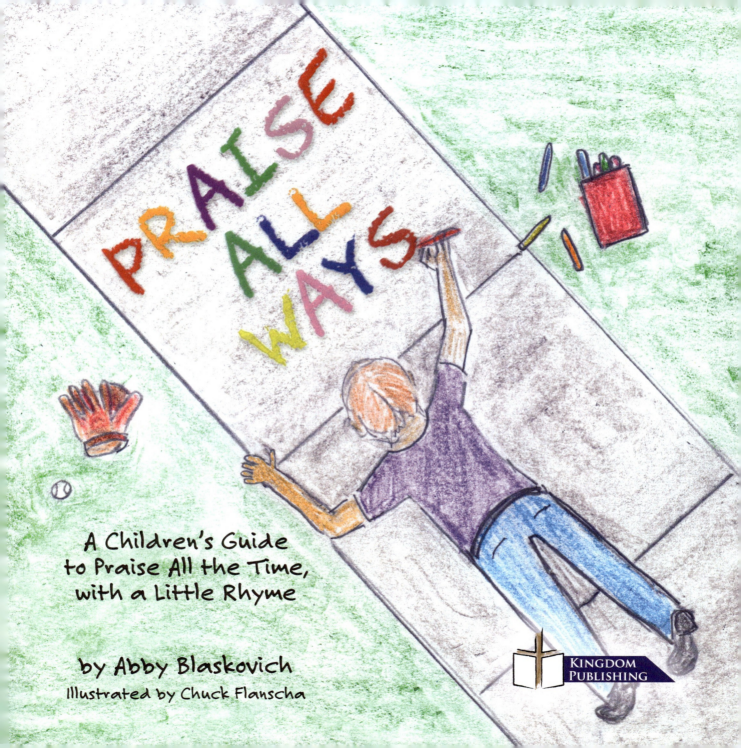

PRAISE ALL WAYS

A Children's Guide
to Praise All the Time,
with a Little Rhyme

by Abby Blaskovich

Illustrated by Chuck Flanscha

KINGDOM PUBLISHING

PRAISE ALL WAYS

A Children's Guide to Praise All the Time,
with a Little Rhyme

by Abby Blaskovich

Illustrated by Chuck Flanscha

KINGDOM PUBLISHING

Kingdom Publishing, LLC
PO Box 630443 • Highlands Ranch, CO 80163
www.Kingdom-Publishing.com

ISBN 978-1-7375156-2-3 (hardcover)
ISBN 978-1-7375156-3-0 (ebook)

Written by Abby Blaskovich
Illustrated by Chuck Flanscha

Names: Blaskovich, Abby, author. | Flanscha, Chuck, illustrator.
Title: Praise all ways : a children's guide to praise all the time , with a little rhyme / by Abby
Blaskovich; illustrated by Chuck Flanscha.
Description: Lone Tree, CO: Kingdom Publishing, LLC, 2022. | Summary: A playful guide to
teach children how to praise God in everyday activities and in all situations.
Identifiers: ISBN: 978-1-7375156-2-3 (hardcover) | 978-1-7375156-3-0 (ebook)
Subjects: LCSH Christian children--Prayers and devotions. | Prayer books and devotions--
Juvenile literature. | Christian life--Juvenile literature. | BISAC JUVENILE NONFICTION / Religious
/ Christian / Devotional & Prayer
Classification: LCC BV4870 .B53 2022 | DDC 242/.62--dc23

Dedication

This book is dedicated to Jackson, Charlie & Lydia –
May you always find something to praise God for
because you are deeply loved by the eternal God.

So, what do we do with this wonderful news?

How do we express this new point-of-view?

It's really quite simple, it all starts with you!

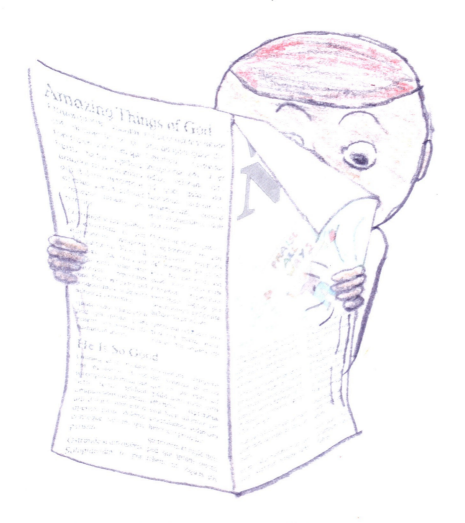

Now listen closely and you will find
that praising God is an everyday rhyme.

You can praise Him in the car.

You can praise Him on a star.

You can praise Him at your school,

and when you're jumping in a pool!

You can praise Him
    when you're trusting.

You can praise Him
    when you're dusting.

You can praise Him when you're perfecting,

and when you're very busy collecting.

You can praise Him
    when you're shaking.

You can praise Him when you're making.

You can praise Him when you're proud,

and when you're being downright loud!

You can praise Him
when you're crying.

You can praise Him
when you're trying.

You can praise Him
        when you're sick,

and when you hear
        the clock tick.

You can praise Him when you're sleepy.

You can praise Him when you pee-pee.

You can praise Him
when you're lonely,

and when you're eating macaroni!

You can praise Him
when you're snuggling.

You can praise Him
when you're struggling.

You can praise Him on a train,
and when you're jetting on a plane.

You can praise Him
	when you're raging.

You can praise Him
	when you're aging.

You can praise Him in the tub,

and when you're diving in a sub!

You can praise Him
        when you're brushing.

You can praise Him when you're rushing.

You can praise Him
when you're
waaaaiting,

and each time you're creating.

You can praise Him
    when you're caring.

You can praise Him when you're daring.

You can praise Him when you're gazing,

when it's all just

SOOOO

AMAZING!

So, you see my dear,
    to praise is not that hard.

You can even praise God when
        you're eating
            Swiss chard!

And when you're praying, praise Him some more,

because God has loved
you always . . .

today . . .

and forever more.

Did you know the Bible is full of praises?
Here are just a few of those holy phrases.

Exodus 15:2
The LORD is my strength and my song, and he has become my salvation; this is my God, and I will praise him, my father's God, and I will exalt him. - Moses

1 Chronicles 16:9
Sing to him, sing praises to him; tell of all his wondrous works! - The Levite Priests

Psalm 57:2
I cry out to God Most High, to God who fulfills his purpose for me. - David

Psalm 88:1-2
O LORD, God of my salvation,
    I cry out day and night before you.
Let my prayer come before you;
    incline your ear to my cry!
- The Sons of Korah

Psalm 98:4
Make a joyful noise to the LORD, all the earth; break forth into joyous song and sing praises! - David

Psalm 113:3
From the rising of the sun to its setting, the name of the LORD is to be praised! - David

Psalm 117:2
For great is his steadfast love toward us, and the faithfulness of the LORD endures forever. Praise the LORD! - Unknown

Psalm 139:14
I praise you, for I am fearfully and wonderfully made. Wonderful are your works; my soul knows it very well. - David

Psalm 145:2
Every day I will bless you and praise your name forever and ever. - David

Psalm 150:1-3
Praise the LORD! Praise God in his sanctuary; praise him in his mighty heavens! Praise him for his mighty deeds; praise him according to his excellent greatness! Praise him with trumpet sound; praise him with lute and harp! - David

Isaiah 12:5

Sing praises to the LORD, for he has done gloriously; let this be made known in all the earth. - Isaiah

Matthew 21:15-16

But when the chief priests and the scribes saw the wonderful things that he did, and the children crying out in the temple, "Hosanna to the Son of David!" they were indignant, and they said to him, "Do you hear what these are saying?" And Jesus said to them, "Yes; have you never read,

"'Out of the mouth of infants and nursing babies you have prepared praise'?" - Jesus

Luke 18:43

And immediately he recovered his sight and followed him, glorifying God. And all the people, when they saw it, gave praise to God. - Luke

Luke 19:40

He answered, "I tell you, if these were silent, the very stones would cry out." - Jesus

1 Corinthians 14:15

What am I to do? I will pray with my spirit, but I will pray with my mind also; I will sing praise with my spirit, but I will sing with my mind also. - Paul

Philippians 4:8

Finally, brothers, whatever is true, whatever is honorable, whatever is just, whatever is pure, whatever is lovely, whatever is commendable, if there is any excellence, if there is anything worthy of praise, think about these things. - Paul

Revelation 19:5

And from the throne came a voice saying, "Praise our God, all you his servants, you who fear him, small and great." - John

One Last Thing...

If *Praise All Ways* has made an impact on you or your family, please visit any online bookstore or GoodReads.com, search for this book and leave a review. It would also be an honor if you share this book on any of your social media pages. Your review does make a difference in helping others find this resource.

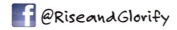 @RiseandGlorify

About the Author

Abby Blaskovich was born in Wisconsin and grew up in a small town in southeastern Colorado. After college, she pursued a career in architecture. Upon starting a family, she and her husband felt called that she be at home full-time with their children. She has settled in Littleton, CO with her husband, three kids, two dogs and one cat. Abby has hidden talents like fully making a bed in record time, and speeding down a drag strip in a racecar. Her loves are Jesus, family and community. Her passions are serving, designing, creating, photography and being the Chief Operating Officer of her home.

About the Illustrator

Chuck Flanscha was born and raised in Wisconsin. He has been married to his wife, Star, for fifty years. They live in rural southeastern Colorado and have four children and eleven grandchildren. Their family hobby is drag racing.

Chuck has enjoyed drawing his entire life. At one point, he considered becoming a commercial artist. However, taking a different path allowed him to become a "jack of many trades." His first job at age twelve, was delivering the morning paper. It proved to be a challenging venture during the Wisconsin winters. He rode his bicycle even in sub-zero temperatures and when finished, he would stop by the City Hall to warm up near the basement furnace before heading home. He has been an over-the-road truck driver, a motel owner/operator and a volunteer fire fighter/EMT. He is also a Vietnam Veteran.

Life came full circle for him when his daughter, Abby, asked him to illustrate her first book.

What People are Saying

In a world full of worry and ingratitude, *Praise All Ways* is the perfect antidote to remind children of all the opportunities to praise God no matter what. Children will love the sing-song rhymes and fun scenarios. This book belongs in every classroom and every home!

- Rachael Mogle
Former preschool teacher, nanny, writer, and mom

. . . .

Seeing God's blessings in our lives through every circumstance can be challenging at times. This book helps open the door for our youth to always find something to praise God for. It helps unlock the childlike faith we are called to have, knowing we have a Father in Heaven that loves us. Practicing how to praise and worship King Jesus is essential!

- Luke Hochevar
Former MLB Player, Unlimited Potential Inc.

. . . .

This is a groundbreaking book in the area of opening the door for parents and their children to have meaningful conversations about their faith and about God.

- Kevin Parker
Former State Representative, small business owner,
father and foster parent

. . . .

What a blessing to young families everywhere! In *Praise All Ways*, Abby Blaskovich encourages children to praise God in everyday ways, helping them build an authentic relationship with their creator. She takes what could be an abstract or daunting idea and makes it practical, and more importantly, **FUN!**

- Taryn Lancaster
Mom of 3 and owner of Sweet Charity Clothing Co.

. . . .

A message that will stand the test of time. So simple, yet profound. Praise Him. Yes, praise Him in all we do. A childlike faith is sometimes the most necessary. Kudos to the author and beautiful illustrations for taking us there on a guided journey.

- J.D. Dudycha
Best-selling author of the *Gage Finley* Series

. . . .

This beautifully illustrated children's book had me smiling and laughing with each rhyme. Our children need this challenge to praise God in every part of their lives.

- Trudy K Swain
Co-Founder, Save Our Youth Mentoring, Denver, CO

. . . .

Visit Abby's Online Shop

Abby is on a mission to encourage you and empower you to live out your God-given purpose. Through her photography on greeting cards and scripture cards, thoughtful books bundles and home decor, you can rise each day and glorify.

Rise + Glorify
Encouragement for Every Day
Empowerment for Life

With the completion of her first book, Abby is now a published author! Be on the lookout for more books from her in the future.

Visit Abby's Facebook business page and Etsy shop at:
www.facebook.com/RiseandGlorify
www.etsy.com/shop/RiseandGlorify

CPSIA information can be obtained
at www.ICGtesting.com
Printed in the USA
LVRC081206020422
714616LV00033B/263